GRANITE AND OTHER IGNEOUS ROCKS

Nancy Kelly Allen

PowerKiDS press™

New York

For Ryan

Published in 2009 by The Rosen Publishing Group, Inc.
29 East 21st Street, New York, NY 10010

First Edition

Editor: Amelie von Zumbusch
Book Design: Kate Laczynski
Photo Researcher: Jessica Gerweck

Photo Credits: Cover, pp. 1, 14 © Getty Images, Inc.; pp. 4, 6, 8, 12, 18 Shutterstock.com; p. 10 © G. Brad Lewis/Getty Images, Inc; p. 16 © Lester Lefkowitz/Getty Images, Inc; p. 20 © Ed Reschke/ Peter Arnold, Inc.

Library of Congress Cataloging-in-Publication Data

Allen, Nancy Kelly, 1949–
    Granite and other igneous rocks / Nancy Kelly Allen. — 1st ed.
        p. cm. — (Rock it!)
Includes index.
    ISBN 978-1-4358-2758-5 (library binding) — ISBN 978-1-4358-3181-0 (pbk.)
ISBN 978-1-4358-3187-2 (6-pack)
    1. Rocks, Igneous—Juvenile literature. I. Title.
    QE461.A548 2009
    552'.1—dc22
                                        2008030095

Manufactured in the United States of America

CPSIA Compliance Information: Batch# CR105010PK: For further information contact Rosen Publishing, New York, New York at 1-800-237-9932.

CONTENTS

Granite rocks, such as these ones in the African country of Namibia, are igneous rocks. Granite forms deep inside Earth.

Rocks Inside and Out

Can you imagine rocks so hot that they melt? Deep inside Earth, it is hot enough to melt rocks. Sometimes this hot, melted rock gets trapped next to solid rocks. Slowly, the melted rock cools and hardens into a kind of rock called igneous rock. The word "igneous" comes from the Latin word *ignis*, which means "fire."

Igneous rocks form above ground, too. Earth's **surface** has weak places in it. Sometimes **volcanoes** form at these weak spots. Hot, melted rock pushes up through the volcanoes and flows out over Earth's surface. When this melted rock cools and hardens, it forms igneous rocks.

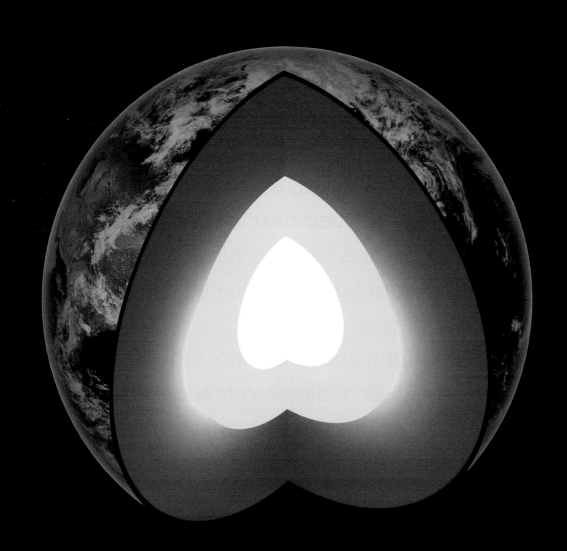

You can see Earth's four layers in this picture.
The crust is the thin, dark, outside layer.
The mantle is shown in red, the outer core
in yellow, and the inner core in white.

Hot to the Core

All igneous rocks begin as melted rock, called **magma**. Magma forms beneath Earth's surface. Earth is made up of four **layers**. The top layer is the crust. Below the crust are the mantle, the **outer** core, and the **inner** core. The crust is broken into large, thick plates made of rock. The plates move around slowly over the mantle. Some of Earth's magma forms at places where the plates rub together.

Most magma forms in Earth's mantle. The mantle is very hot. In fact, it is generally between 2,912° F and 7,232° F (1,600–4,000° C) there! There is also a lot of **pressure** in the mantle. The high heat and pressure make some of the mantle's rock melt into magma.

Popocatépetl, in Mexico, is North America's second-largest volcano. It is 17,800 feet (5,425 m) tall.

Exploding Volcanoes

Magma does not always stay in the mantle. Sometimes, the plates that make up Earth's crust pull apart or rub together to form volcanoes. Heat and pressure from inside Earth push magma through these volcanoes. Once the magma reaches Earth's surface, it is called lava.

Volcanoes occur in different sizes and shapes. Some are cone-shaped mountains. Others are long breaks in the ground. Some volcanoes shoot lava high into the air in showy explosions. Lava flows slowly out of others. There are even underwater volcanoes! All kinds of volcanoes produce igneous rock.

Earth has about 800 active volcanoes. There are 700 more volcanoes that might some day become active. Many of Earth's volcanoes circle the Pacific Ocean. This string of volcanoes is called the Ring of Fire.

This pahoehoe is flowing over a beach in the Hawaii Volcanoes National Park. You can already see the wavy surface the pahoehoe will have when it cools.

The Outside Story

Igneous rock that forms outside Earth's crust is called extrusive rock. Lava from volcanoes forms most extrusive rocks. Once the lava leaves the volcano, it cools and hardens quickly. The **minerals** in this fast-cooling lava form small **crystals**. This means that extrusive rocks are generally very smooth.

There are several different kinds of lava. Different kinds of lava produce rocks that look different. For example, underwater volcanoes produce pillow lava. This forms large, rounded lumps of rock. A kind of smoothly moving lava called **pahoehoe** forms bumpy rocks. *Pahoehoe* is a Hawaiian word. It is most often used for lava from Hawaiian volcanoes, such as Kilauea.

Turkey's Goreme National Park is home to rock formations called fairy chimneys. They are made mostly from tuff, but some have basalt tops. In the past, people cut homes in the fairy chimneys.

Solid as a Rock

Several different kinds of rocks form from lava. For example, rhyolite is a kind of rock made from thick lava. This rock has a light color and fine grains. Basalt is the most common type of extrusive igneous rock. Volcanoes that **erupt** on the ocean floor often form basalt rocks. Basalt cools quickly and forms fine grains.

Some volcanoes shoot out hot ash instead of lava. Ash is a powder or dust made of tiny pieces of hardened magma. A soft kind of igneous rock called tuff forms from the ash from volcanic eruptions.

The Giant's Causeway, in Northern Ireland, is made of basalt rock. The rock looks as if it was cut, but it was really formed by a lava flow.

These daggers are made of the igneous rock obsidian. They were produced by the Aztecs, a Native American people who lived in what is now Mexico.

Sharp as a Rock

Igneous rocks can be beautiful. Obsidian is a black or dark red extrusive igneous rock. This rock is a smooth, shiny, natural glass. Like glass, it breaks into pieces that have sharp edges. Obsidian forms when lava cools very quickly. It cools so fast that no crystals form.

Pumice is a very unusual extrusive igneous rock. It forms when lava cools quickly and gases get trapped inside it. The gases form air pockets or small holes. The holes make pumice very light. It is so light that it floats in water!

Long ago, people used obsidian to make tools, such as knife blades. The rock's sharp edges were used for cutting. The shiny rock was also used as a mirror, or looking glass.

The intrusive rock granite is often used for building. This man is cutting building blocks in a granite quarry. Quarries are places where rocks or minerals are taken out of the ground.

The Inside Story

Not all igneous rocks are made by volcanoes. Intrusive igneous rocks form from magma deep inside Earth. These rocks cool and harden very slowly. The slow cooling causes the minerals inside the hardening rocks to form large crystals. These crystals give intrusive igneous rocks a grainy surface.

Intrusive rocks appear on Earth's surface when they are pushed up through the crust or when the rocks above them wear away. This can take **billions** of years. Dolerite, granite, and gabbro are three types of intrusive igneous rocks. Dolerite is a dark rock. It has smaller grains than granite and gabbro do because dolerite cooled more quickly when it formed.

This inuksuk in British Columbia, Canada, is made of granite. An inuksuk is a large stone figure made by the Inuit. The Inuit are a native people of Alaska, Greenland, and northern Canada.

Built to Last

Granite is a common intrusive igneous rock. This rock is made of the minerals quartz, feldspar, and mica. While quartz crystals are clear, mica crystals are dark, and feldspar crystals are white, gray, pink, or yellow. These three minerals give granite a spotted look. Because pieces of granite from different places have different amounts of minerals, granite can come in many colors. Its colors range from gray to red.

Granite is very strong. For that reason, it is often used as a building stone. Buildings made of granite last for many years.

Granite is a building stone used in the Great Wall of China. This huge wall is 4,000 miles (6,437 km) long. Parts of the Great Wall are over 2,500 years old!

The rock behind this waterfall is granite gneiss. Granite gneiss is a kind of metamorphic rock that forms from the igneous rock granite.

Going in Circles

Igneous rocks are just one of Earth's three kinds of rocks. The other two kinds of rocks are called sedimentary rocks and metamorphic rocks. New rocks are always being made from old rocks. This action is called the rock cycle.

Water, wind, and ice break igneous or metamorphic rocks into small pieces called sediment. Over time, layers of sediment build up and harden into sedimentary rock. Heat and pressure inside Earth change igneous and sedimentary rocks to metamorphic rocks. When metamorphic and sedimentary rocks are pushed deep under ground, they melt into magma. In time, this magma may form igneous rocks. The rock cycle never ends.

Rocks All Around

You may not know it, but igneous rocks are all around you. People use these rocks every day. Many strong intrusive igneous rocks, such as granite and gabbro, are used as building stones. These hard rocks also form beautiful landforms that people enjoy visiting and climbing. El Capitan, a huge granite formation in California's Yosemite National Park, is one such landform.

Extrusive igneous rocks are useful, too. Pumice is used to rub dry skin off feet. Basalt is used to surface roads. Igneous rocks are everywhere. You can walk on them, build with them, and collect them. Take a close look at the rocks around you.

GLOSSARY

billions (BIL-yunz) Thousands of millions. One billion is 1,000 millions.

crystals (KRIS-tulz) Pieces of hard, clear matter that have points and flat sides.

erupt (ih-RUPT) To break open or come out.

inner (IN-nur) On the inside.

layers (LAY-erz) Thicknesses of something.

magma (MAG-muh) Hot, melted rock inside Earth.

minerals (MIN-rulz) Natural things that are not animals, plants, or other living things.

outer (OWT-ur) On the outside.

pahoehoe (puh-HOH-ee-hoh-ee) Lava with a smooth, ropelike outside.

pressure (PREH-shur) A force that pushes on something.

surface (SER-fes) The outside of anything.

volcanoes (vol-KAY-nohz) Openings that sometimes shoot up hot, melted rock called lava.

INDEX

WEB SITES

Due to the changing nature of Internet links, PowerKids Press has developed an online list of Web sites related to the subject of this book. This site is updated regularly. Please use this link to access the list:
www.powerkidslinks.com/rockit/granite/